CW01064461

Original title:
Inspire Your Imagination

Editor: Theodor Taimla
Author: Meelis Maurus
ISBN HARDBACK: 978-9916-763-84-1
ISBN PAPERBACK: 978-9916-763-85-8

The Horizon of Fantasy

Beyond the waves of silver seas,
Where dreams take flight on gentle breeze.
The stars align in twinkling dance,
Inviting hearts to take a chance.

Mountains rise and valleys fall,
Echoing whispers, a beckoning call.
In shadows deep, where fairies play,
Imagination lights the way.

A land where wonder never dies,
And every cloud is painted skies.
Each wish a seed in fertile ground,
In twilight's glow, magic is found.

Through forests dense and rivers wide,
Adventure waits, our hearts as guide.
The journey calls, with each new dawn,
A world reborn, where dreams are drawn.

So lift your gaze to the endless night,
Embrace the magic, bask in the light.
For within your heart, a spark shall gleam,
Forevermore, we chase the dream.

Glimmers of Creation

In quiet hours when shadows blend,
A spark ignites, ideas transcend.
Brush strokes dance on fabric bare,
Crafting worlds from whispers rare.

In silence deep, a vision wakes,
The heart inspires, the canvas shakes.
Each color bold, each line a breath,
A testament to life and death.

From chaos born, a beauty swells,
With every thought, the story dwells.
A symphony of light and shade,
In every form, the soul displayed.

Textures mingle, emotions stir,
As dreams transform, the artist's blur.
With each creation, a truth unfolds,
The essence of life, in colors bold.

So seize the night, let visions roam,
In each crafted piece, find a home.
For in creation, we find our play,
Glimmers of hope, come what may.

A Canvas of Dreams

Upon the canvas, visions bloom,
In splashes bright, dispelling gloom.
With every stroke, the heart does sing,
A tale of hopes, the joy they bring.

Colors whisper in a sweet embrace,
As dreams awaken, take their place.
Brush in hand, the spirit soars,
Unveiling wonders, opening doors.

With every hue, a story spun,
Reflections dance, as day is done.
In layers deep, the essence lies,
A symphony beneath the skies.

A patchwork quilt of wishes vast,
Uniting future, present, past.
In every corner, magic gleams,
A canvas painted with our dreams.

So dream anew with every shade,
In this expanse, let fears fade.
The world awaits the joy we bring,
On life's canvas, love takes wing.

Whispers of the Mind

In quiet corners, thoughts take flight,
Whispers echo in the night.
Ideas meld like swirling mist,
In the heart's chambers, we persist.

The mind's a maze, a labyrinth true,
With paths untraveled, old and new.
Each turning point a chance to see,
The whispered secrets, wild and free.

Like moonlit streams that gently flow,
In reflections deep, our visions grow.
What once was fleeting becomes profound,
In whispers soft, we're spellbound.

Through tangled webs of dreams we weave,
A tapestry of hopes we believe.
With every thought, a journey starts,
In the quiet hum of waiting hearts.

So listen close, let visions unwind,
In every shadow, whispers bind.
For in the silence, truth will find,
The beauty held in whispers of the mind.

The Journey Beyond

Through valleys deep and mountains high,
We tread the paths where eagles fly.
With every step, the spirit sings,
The promise of what tomorrow brings.

The river flows, the stars align,
In whispered winds, our souls entwine.
We chase the dawn, embrace the night,
In shadows cast, we find the light.

Across the seas, we drift and roam,
With every heartbeat, we feel at home.
The call of dreams, like waves that swell,
Together, we weave our timeless spell.

In every heart, a song resides,
An echoing truth where hope abides.
With courage strong, we face the tide,
On this wild journey, we will glide.

So let us stand, hand in hand,
And write our tale across the land.
With every choice, our spirits soar,
The journey beyond, forevermore.

Boundless Dreams

In fields where wildflowers dance and play,
The dreamers gather, hearts light as day.
With colors bright, they paint the skies,
Creating worlds with hopeful sighs.

Each whispered thought, a seed of light,
In quiet moments, dreams take flight.
With open hearts, they chase the hues,
Of boundless skies, where hope renews.

Across the mountains, through the trees,
The laughter echoes on the breeze.
In every soul, a vision gleams,
A tapestry woven of their dreams.

Through endless nights and bright tomorrows,
They share their joy, and ease their sorrows.
In bonds unbroken, they gracefully soar,
United in dreams forevermore.

So let us wander, hand in hand,
Through boundless dreams, a timeless land.
With every step, our spirits gleam,
Together we thrive, in love we dream.

The Palette of Tomorrow

Upon the canvas, colors blend,
A vibrant vision we transcend.
With each stroke, a story grows,
In shades of passion, hope flows.

The dawn awakes with golden rays,
In painted skies, the future plays.
With every hue, a dream ignites,
The palette sings of endless nights.

In gentle whispers, art emerges,
From quiet hearts and inner surges.
We blend our fears with courage bold,
In every stroke, a truth unfolds.

The world awaits beneath our hands,
In vivid shades, our spirit stands.
The palette speaks, our hearts entwined,
Creating beauty, one of a kind.

So let us paint with love's embrace,
A canvas rich, a sacred space.
In hues of joy, we'll leave our mark,
The palette of tomorrow, our spark.

Illuminating the Void

In absence felt, a silence deep,
The void invites our hearts to leap.
With flickers bright, we seek to find,
A light that shines within the mind.

Through shadowed paths, we dare to tread,
With hope as guide, no fear or dread.
The stars above, like dreams aglow,
Illuminate the vast unknown.

With every step, we forge a way,
Through darkness thick, we'll not dismay.
In every heartbeat, strength we gain,
Together facing joy and pain.

So cast aside the weight of night,
Embrace the dawn with all your might.
For in the void, a spark remains,
Illuminating life's sweet gains.

With every breath, we rise anew,
In unity, our spirits grew.
Through trials faced, we claim our choice,
Illuminating the void, our voice.

The Catalyst of Curiosity

A whisper in the night,
Awakens dreams untold.
Questions dance in moonlight,
Seeking tales of old.

Wandering through the maze,
Of thoughts that ebb and flow.
Each corner sparks a blaze,
Of wonder's soft glow.

In the heart of the quest,
Truths reveal their embrace.
Exploration's sweet jest,
Leads us to our place.

With every step we take,
The world unfurls again.
Curiosity's wake,
Informs the soul of men.

So let the spark ignite,
Let knowledge take its flight.
For in the curious heart,
Is where all journeys start.

The Haiku of Possibility

In silence it breathes,
A dream not yet fulfilled,
Nature's soft embrace.

The dawn paints the skies,
With colors of the heart.
Hope whispers its song.

Every step we take,
Into the great unknown,
Paths unveil their truth.

Beneath the still trees,
A promise gently stirs,
Fields of shining light.

Endless wings shall soar,
On winds of open chance,
Life's dance, wild and free.

Light Amidst Shadows

In the twilight's glow,
A flicker starts to rise,
Hope defies the dark,
With dreams that fill the skies.

Through the tangled woods,
Where shadows often creep,
A courage ignites,
In depths, secrets sleep.

Stars pierce the black night,
Like truths that break the chains,
Each spark a beacon,
Amidst the lost remains.

With whispers of light,
We carve a brighter way,
The shadows retreat,
At the dawn of day.

In every heart beats,
A flame that knows no bound,
In light, we find strength,
And unity is found.

The Visionary's Forge

In the fires of thought,
A spark begins to shine,
Minds shape the future,
Like steel turned divine.

Crafting dreams with care,
Each stroke a brave design,
Visions take their flight,
In rhythms so aligned.

Through trials and tests,
The heart learns to be bold,
With courage as guide,
New stories unfold.

In the depths of night,
Ideas are reborn,
The visionary's gift,
A light for the worn.

From ashes to grace,
In creation we trust,
Forging paths of hope,
In obsidian dust.

Threads of the Surreal

In shadows deep, the whispers play,
Entangled dreams in light's ballet.
A tapestry of thoughts unwound,
In every corner, oddities are found.

Cascading colors twist and weave,
Where reality dares to conceive.
A world that's slightly out of tune,
Beneath the laughter of the moon.

Echoes echo in silent void,
Fleeting moments, never enjoyed.
Time drips slowly, like morning dew,
In the surreal, all feels anew.

Faces shift like clouds in flight,
Haunting visions in the night.
A gentle tug on seams of fate,
In this realm, we create, relate.

Fragments dance in endless loop,
A whimsical and curious group.
Weaving tales without a seam,
In threads of the surreal, we dream.

The Dreamweaver's Muse

With gentle hands, she spins the night,
Crafting dreams in purest light.
A tapestry where hopes ignite,
In silence woven, ever bright.

With every stitch, a tale unfolds,
Of brave adventures and treasures bold.
Where fantasies take flight and soar,
In the heart of the dreamweaver's lore.

Soft whispers guide the hearts that roam,
Through vivid lands that feel like home.
In her embrace, night's magic grows,
Each thread a wish that softly glows.

She catches sighs in her delicate weave,
In worlds where souls still believe.
Every slumber holds a key,
To unlock doors of mystery.

So close your eyes and drift away,
Into realms where shadows play.
In the hands of the dreamweaver's muse,
Embrace the night, where dreams amuse.

Colliding Worlds

Two realms collide in cosmic dance,
A meeting born of fate and chance.
Where stars align and echoes sing,
In chaos, beauty starts to spring.

An ancient clash of night and day,
A spectrum where the lost can stray.
Across the void, a bridge displayed,
In collision, worlds are made.

Mountains rise with oceans deep,
In every fold, a secret keeps.
The clash of light, the dark's embrace,
In every corner, time finds space.

A dance of shadows, hints of gold,
Each moment breathes a tale untold.
In colliding rhythms, fate entwined,
A union of the heart and mind.

So wander on in this vast expanse,
Where echoes linger in a trance.
For in collision, life finds worth,
Two worlds united, in rebirth.

The Canvas of the Night

Stretched across the velvet sky,
Stars are painted, shining high.
A canvas rich with dreams and sighs,
In the stillness, imagination flies.

With every stroke, the moonbeams glow,
Splashing silver on the dark below.
A brush dipped in midnight hues,
Crafting visions we can choose.

The whispers of the breeze, a song,
Guiding us where we belong.
In this gallery of endless dreams,
Reality fades; nothing's as it seems.

Each twinkle tells a story bold,
Of wishes cast and secrets told.
In twilight hours, the magic grows,
The canvas of the night bestows.

So let your heart be filled with light,
In this vast, enchanting night.
With every heartbeat, colors blend,
On the canvas where dreams transcend.

Blossoms of Inspiration

In gardens wide, ideas bloom,
Petals bright chase away the gloom.
Sunlight spills on thoughts up high,
In whispers soft, like a sigh.

The breeze carries tales untold,
Of dreams once birthed, now brave and bold.
Each moment crafted with intent,
A canvas fresh, a heart's content.

Amidst the thorns, we find our way,
A spark ignites at break of day.
With every stroke, our spirits rise,
In colors bright, we paint the skies.

Nature hums a gentle tune,
Underneath the silver moon.
Inspiring hearts to take their flight,
Turning shadows into light.

So dance among these vibrant hues,
Embrace the magic, chase your muse.
For in this space, the world is free,
A blossom waits for you and me.

The Dance of Epiphanies

Whispers linger in the air,
Moments flash, so bright, so rare.
Like twinkling stars that guide the night,
Each spark ignites with pure delight.

Steps untaken, paths unknown,
In quiet corners, truth is sown.
A rhythm sways, our hearts align,
In swirling dreams, we intertwine.

From shadows deep, a light will break,
With every choice, new futures make.
A dance of thoughts, a leap of faith,
These epiphanies, we embrace.

In the stillness, wisdom's near,
Echoes whisper, loud and clear.
Each revelation, a sacred chance,
To join the world in cosmic dance.

Embrace the pulse of dawn's first light,
Let insight guide through day and night.
For in this dance, we find our way,
To treasures waiting, come what may.

Whimsical Wanderlust

Underneath the endless sky,
Adventures call, our spirits fly.
With every step, the world unfolds,
In colors vibrant, stories told.

Through winding paths where rivers sing,
Every moment feels like spring.
Curious hearts chase the unknown,
In lands where seeds of dreams are sown.

Whispers of the ocean breeze,
Lead us to the swaying trees.
Where laughter dances with the sun,
In this journey, we are one.

Maps are drawn with strokes of fate,
We ride the waves, we celebrate.
In every corner, life's a quest,
To seek the heart, we're truly blessed.

So pack your dreams, let courage reign,
In wandering souls, there is no pain.
Together we'll embrace the vast,
In whimsical paths, our shadows cast.

Fragments of a Bright Tomorrow

Scattered pieces in the light,
Dreams emerge from darkest night.
Hope, like stars, will always shine,
With every heartbeat, love aligns.

In moments paused, reflection waits,
New beginnings at the gates.
Let go of fears that hold us tight,
Embrace the dawn, ignite the night.

Together we can weave the seams,
Of brighter days and bolder dreams.
With every challenge, we'll ignite,
The fire within, our spirits bright.

Fragments whisper, softly tread,
In every doubt, a seed is spread.
With open hearts, we'll find our way,
Towards a brighter, better day.

So take my hand, let's forge ahead,
With every step, our hopes are fed.
For in the pieces, truth we'll find,
A tomorrow crafted, intertwined.

The Spark Beneath the Surface

In quiet depths, a flicker glows,
A whisper of dreams, where silence grows.
Hidden treasures lie in wait,
Nurtured by time, a gentle fate.

Beneath the waves, the currents sway,
Fueling the fire that lights the way.
Each heartbeat echoes, wild and free,
An ember's warmth, the soul's decree.

Beneath the calm, a storm does build,
With hopes aflame, our spirits thrilled.
Unseen forces guide the night,
As shadows dance in fading light.

And in the dark, the spark ignites,
Illumination through the heights.
From depths unknown, behold the sight,
A glimmer born from endless night.

So trust the spark that lies within,
The journey starts where dreams begin.
In every heart, a flame can thrive,
Embrace the light, and feel alive.

Lighting the Imagination

A canvas wide, with stars to trace,
Brush strokes of thought, in endless space.
Color the dreams that twirl and spin,
Awakening visions deep within.

Words like lanterns guide the way,
Igniting shadows that dare to stay.
Each flicker brightens what we see,
The magic held in fantasy.

Ideas burst like fireworks bright,
Creating worlds in the still of night.
In every heart, a story waits,
Unlock the door, open the gates.

So let your mind take flight and glide,
Across the realms where wonders hide.
With every spark, a tale unfolds,
In the realm of dreams, be bold.

For in the space where thoughts collide,
New worlds emerge, no need to hide.
Embrace the light, let it unfurl,
Ignite your dreams, transform your world.

Embracing the Unseen

In shadows cast by distant stars,
Lie secrets held in silent bars.
Whispers soft, like ghosts of night,
Invite us in, through hidden light.

Each breath we take, a bridge to grace,
Where time bends slow, in quiet space.
The unseen threads that weave us near,
Connect our hearts, dissolve the fear.

For in the depths, the silence speaks,
In every pause, the universe seeks.
Embrace the hidden, draw it close,
For in the dark, the spirit grows.

The uncharted paths, we dare to roam,
In the unknown, we find our home.
So let the mystery be your guide,
And brave the night, with light inside.

For in the unseen, treasures gleam,
Awakening the heart's pure dream.
Embrace the magic, let it sway,
And trust the journey, come what may.

Chasing Epiphanies

As dawn breaks forth, a moment shines,
The world awakens, and thought aligns.
Eureka whispers through the haze,
Igniting minds in vibrant blaze.

With every thought, a spark ignites,
Illuminating shadowed sights.
The chase begins, as questions rise,
An endless quest, beneath the skies.

Winding paths through tangled dreams,
Unravel truths, or so it seems.
Each epiphany, a treasure found,
In every turn, new grounds abound.

The heart races, the pulse ignites,
As clarity blooms in daylight's bites.
With each discovery, wisdom flows,
In every answer, a mystery grows.

So chase the thoughts that set you free,
In every heartbeat, seek to be.
For the journey leads where few have gone,
In the dance of light, we journey on.

The Symphony of Colors

A canvas spreads wide and bright,
Where hues of laughter dance in light.
Crimson whispers with a dream,
While sapphire sings of the serene.

Golden rays kiss the morning dew,
Emerald leaves in vibrant view.
Each stroke a tale, a silent sound,
In the palette where joy is found.

Indigo skies wrap the night,
With silver stars that shimmer bright.
A symphony played on the breeze,
Nature's art that aims to please.

Pastel clouds drift softly by,
As twilight paints a gentle sigh.
In every shade, a heartbeat flows,
Each color tells what beauty knows.

So let us dance in hues so bold,
With every story yet untold.
In the symphony of shades we trust,
A vibrant world of dreams and dust.

Fables of the Heart

In whispers soft, the heart reveals,
Tales of love that fate conceals.
With every beat, a story spins,
Embracing all the loss and wins.

Hopeful laughter in the night,
Guiding souls to find the light.
Every moment, woven tight,
A fable born from joy and flight.

Through storms that rattle, dreams take wing,
In silence felt, the spirit sings.
Embers glow in shadows cast,
Fables of the heart hold fast.

Fragments of a tender vow,
In every glance, the world knows how.
Each chapter penned in gentle grace,
Stories told, love's warm embrace.

Through trials faced and paths unknown,
The heart's true fable is grown.
In every tear, in every smile,
Lies the journey, the sacred mile.

The Art of Unfolding

Like petals soft in morning light,
Life unfolds, a wondrous sight.
In layers deep, hidden so well,
The art of knowing, stories to tell.

Time whispers secrets, gently shared,
Each moment cherished, deeply cared.
In every breath, a chance to grow,
Revealing parts we scarcely know.

Patience paints a richer scene,
With every challenge, we glean.
Through trials faced, we learn to bend,
The art of folding, changes mend.

In twilight's glow, reflecting back,
The path revealed in hues intact.
With courage held and hearts so bold,
Each unfolding, a story told.

So cherish time, let moments bloom,
In life's sweet dance, dispel the gloom.
For in the art of letting be,
We find the truth, our legacy.

Chasing Starlight

In the quiet of the night,
Dreamers reach for endless light.
With open hearts, they take the flight,
Chasing starlight, bold and bright.

Whispers swirl in the velvet air,
Promises strung like jewels so rare.
Each sparkle holds a wish, a prayer,
Guiding wanderers, everywhere.

Through the shadows, hope will gleam,
Igniting faith in every dream.
A cosmic dance, a timeless theme,
Chasing starlight, a heart's sweet beam.

Every twinkle, a tale of old,
Stories of the brave and bold.
In constellations bright and wide,
The night reveals what hearts confide.

So when the dawn begins to break,
And dreams dissolve like morning flake,
Remember the glimmer in your soul,
Chasing starlight makes you whole.

Kaleidoscope of Visions

In colors bright, we wander wide,
Shifting shapes, where dreams collide.
A swirl of thoughts, both strange and clear,
We chase the whispers only we hear.

Through every turn, a brand new sight,
Fragments dance in morning light.
A glimpse of futures, hopes untold,
In every pattern, a story unfolds.

With every blink, the world's anew,
Creativity flows like morning dew.
The heart ignites with visions bold,
In the kaleidoscope, we find our gold.

Threads of Enchantment

In twilight's glow, the fibers weave,
Enchanting tales that we believe.
With every stitch, a memory sewn,
In vibrant hues, our dreams are blown.

Through silver lines, our laughter spins,
Binding hearts where love begins.
A tapestry that time bestows,
In every thread, our magic grows.

With gentle hands, we craft our fate,
In every knot, the whispered state.
Through strands of hope, we find our way,
In threads of enchantment, we will stay.

Dancing with Ideas

In midnight air, ideas take flight,
They swirl and twirl in sheer delight.
From quiet thoughts, the visions spring,
A vibrant dance, where spirits sing.

With every turn, new pathways beat,
In rhythm soft, the mind's retreat.
Bold concepts leap from heart to mind,
In this grand waltz, the free unwind.

As shadows fade, the echoes call,
In unity, we share it all.
Together we sway, a fearless team,
In dancing vows, we chase the dream.

The Magic of Daydreams

Beneath the sun, our thoughts abide,
In fleecy clouds, where hopes reside.
With every glance, the world expands,
In gentle strokes, the mind commands.

A ship of dreams on seas so wide,
Caught in the winds of thoughts inside.
With every wave, we brave the new,
In daydreams deep, our spirits grew.

A fleeting moment, a spark of light,
In daydream's realm, we take our flight.
From whispered hopes to radiant beams,
In the heart, we cradle our dreams.

Castles in the Air

In dreams we build them high,
Where clouds and sunlight play.
With laughter, hopes draw nigh,
In colors bright as day.

Each tower holds a wish,
A latticework of gold.
We ride on winds that swish,
With hearts both brave and bold.

Beneath the moonlit glow,
We dance upon the breeze.
Our secrets softly flow,
Like whispers through the trees.

In shadows, stories hide,
Of realms we've yet to see.
With faith as our true guide,
We'll craft our destiny.

So let us soar so high,
With visions ever bright.
For in the endless sky,
We make our dreams take flight.

The Breath of Inventiveness

In silence, sparks ignite,
A thought begins to bloom.
With colors pure and bright,
We banish all the gloom.

Ideas leap and dance,
Like fireflies in the night.
Each moment, a new chance,
To weave the dark with light.

With hands that grasp the stars,
We mold the world anew.
In galaxies afar,
Our visions break right through.

In chaos, we find peace,
A formula divine.
With every piece, release,
As art and science twine.

So let the mind take flight,
Inventive, bold we stand.
With dreams that shine so bright,
We dare to change the land.

A Symphony of the Soul

Notes rise like morning light,
In harmony they weave.
Each chord a gentle flight,
A tapestry to leave.

With rhythm in our hearts,
We dance through joy and pain.
Each moment, piece imparts,
The beauty from our strain.

In whispers, echoes flow,
Resonating through time.
A melody we know,
Our spirits start to climb.

With every sound we make,
We join the cosmic song.
From silence, we awake,
Where all of us belong.

So let the music soar,
Unbound and ever free.
A symphony we pour,
From souls in harmony.

The Quill and the Dreamer

A quill in hand, we roam,
Through worlds both far and near.
With ink, we find our home,
In tales that we hold dear.

Each stroke, a spark of light,
A dance of words on page.
With dreams, we take to flight,
The heart becomes the stage.

In whispered fantasies,
We share our fears and hopes.
With every tale that frees,
Our spirit gently copes.

From shadows, stories soar,
In verses, love and loss.
We craft forevermore,
Through joy and through the cross.

So let the words unfold,
With magic yet untold.
The quill, a wand of gold,
For dreamers brave and bold.

Boundless Horizons

Waves crash upon the shore,
Endless skies meet the sea.
Dreamers gaze forevermore,
Seeking where they long to be.

Mountains rise to touch the blue,
Whispers carried on the breeze.
Paths unfold for me and you,
Nature's canvas, hearts at ease.

Sunsets paint a golden hue,
Stars emerge as day does fade.
In the vastness, hope shines through,
Each heartbeat, a serenade.

Across the land, horizons call,
Adventures waiting to unfold.
Together we will rise and fall,
In stories yet to be told.

Boundless dreams take flight and soar,
In the realms where shadows play.
With each step, we yearn for more,
Chasing night, embracing day.

The Colors of Thought

In fields of vibrant hues we roam,
Each petal whispers tales untold.
Brushstrokes dance, creating home,
With every color, dreams unfold.

Mind's palette rich, emotions blend,
Sparks of genius shine so bright.
Ideas flow, they twist and bend,
In the silence, find the light.

Crimson passion fuels the fire,
Indigo depth, the soul ignites.
Golden hopes reach ever higher,
In the dark, revealing sights.

From twilight grey to dawn's warm pink,
Each thought a canvas yet to paint.
In swirling shades, we stop to think,
Creating worlds, free of restraint.

Let colors burst, let visions thrive,
In this spectacle of light.
In every shade, new dreams arrive,
Through colors of depth and delight.

Echoes of Creativity

In the stillness, echoes call,
Whispers weave through time and space.
In each heartbeat, dreams stand tall,
Imagination finds its place.

Brush in hand, we start to flow,
Ink spills words upon the page.
Crafting worlds, we'll watch them grow,
Each line, a dance, a timeless stage.

Notes arise, a symphony,
Melodies in the air collide.
From silence blooms such harmony,
In the rhythm, we abide.

With each spark, a vision spreads,
Creative flames ignite the night.
From vibrant dreams, our passion treads,
Chasing shadows, chasing light.

Together, let the echoes ring,
In every heart, the muse arrives.
Through art and song, we take to wing,
In creativity, our spirit thrives.

Flights of Fancy

Upon the breeze, we take to flight,
Wings unfurl in softest grace.
Chasing clouds with pure delight,
Lost in dreams, in time and space.

With every thought, our hearts take wing,
Soaring high, we laugh and play.
In this moment, we are kings,
Freedom blooms in bright array.

Floating softly, weightless glee,
Through sunlit rays and starlit skies.
In the winds of possibility,
Imagination never dies.

Dreaming realms, both far and near,
Every vision whispers bold.
Through flights of fancy, we draw near,
To treasures waiting to be told.

As daylight dims and shadows sigh,
We glide through twilight's gentle glow.
In our hearts, we'll always fly,
Wherever dreams and wonders flow.

The Unseen Tapestry

Threads of fate weave through the night,
Colors blend, a dance of light.
Whispers soft, in shadows deep,
Stories linger, secrets keep.

Silken dreams drift on the breeze,
Echoes brush against the trees.
Patterns form, both bold and faint,
Silent whispers of a saint.

Woven tales, both new and old,
Every strand, a tale retold.
In the weave, the heart finds peace,
In the quiet, joys increase.

Threads entwined, the dark and bright,
Fractals gleam in silver light.
Each connection, love's embrace,
In this world, we find our place.

As I wander through the night,
The unseen holds pure delight.
In my heart, the tapestry,
Maps the soul's own mystery.

Reveries at Dusk

As the sun dips low to rest,
The horizon wears its best.
Colors wash the evening sky,
A symphony of soft goodbye.

Whispers of the coming night,
Echoes of the fading light.
Dreams arise on the cool air,
Hopes reflected everywhere.

In the stillness, thoughts collide,
Imagination's gentle ride.
Butterflies of memory flit,
In this moment, all is fit.

Crickets sing, their lullabies,
Starlight dances in the eyes.
Nature's canvas, wide and vast,
In this moment, time is cast.

Let the twilight take its hold,
Stories of the night unfold.
In reveries, we lose our way,
Finding peace at the end of day.

A Symphony of Whimsy

In a world of vibrant dreams,
Magic flows in silver streams.
Laughter bubbles, colors swirl,
Every heart begins to twirl.

Pixies dance on moonlit beams,
Whispers float, a dance of gleams.
Silly thoughts take flight and soar,
Imagination opens doors.

Collecting stardust in a jar,
Every wish is not too far.
With a sprinkle and a grin,
Joyful chaos can begin.

Tales of wonder weave with grace,
Every moment, a new place.
In the realms where dreams collide,
A symphony we cannot hide.

Winds of whimsy guide our way,
In this magic, we will stay.
Let the tunes of laughter play,
In this realm, we'll find our sway.

The Gateway to Possibility

Upon the rise of dawn's embrace,
Lies a path of boundless space.
Every choice a step in time,
A new journey, a new rhyme.

Windows open to the sky,
Wings of hope begin to fly.
Paths diverge in bright array,
Each one beckoning, "Come play!"

In the whispers of the morn,
New dreams blossom, hope reborn.
Every moment, take a chance,
In the light, let spirits dance.

What lies beyond, we cannot know,
In the heart, the seeds will grow.
Each decision, a doorway wide,
Into worlds where dreams reside.

Beyond the gate, the truth remains,
In our hands, the path contains.
Trust the journey, let it be,
The gateway holds eternity.

Journeys Beyond Reality

Through misty paths we tread alone,
In dreams where shadows softly moan.
The stars align with whispered grace,
As time unwinds in a timeless space.

With every step, we chase the light,
Eclipsing fears that lurk in night.
The mind expands in a boundless flow,
To places where only visions go.

As tales unfold on woven air,
A dance of echoes, a cosmic fair.
We glide on wings of fleeting thought,
In realms where every truth is sought.

To fade away from all we know,
Into the currents, lost and flow.
Where yesterday and tomorrow blend,
And every journey leads to mend.

So find your heart in the great unknown,
Embrace the worlds you can call your own.
For in each step, the universe sings,
And in our quest, eternity springs.

Unveiling the Hidden

Beneath the layers of everyday,
Lies a truth that yearns to play.
In whispers lost to time and space,
We seek the light, we crave the grace.

With each small crack, the secrets breathe,
In shadows where the lost believe.
We peel away the masks of fate,
To find the dreams that hesitate.

In corners dark, the stories twine,
With echoes sharp, like crispest wine.
We chase the threads of ancient lore,
Unlocking doors forevermore.

The quest begins with silent oaths,
To bring forth what our spirit broths.
The hidden gems of thought unspooled,
In vast expanses, once concealed.

So let us wander, open eyes,
To find the truth where silence lies.
Together we'll unveil, ignite,
The beauty that resides in night.

The Resonance of Ideas

In echoes formed by hearts and minds,
Resonance hums, with power it binds.
A thought takes flight, a whisper grows,
In unity, the vision flows.

The spark ignites, we stand as one,
In dialogue, the work begun.
Ideas dance in vibrant hues,
In shared belief, the world renews.

From distant shores, we gather round,
In every voice, a sacred sound.
Through open hearts, the future's bright,
In every word, we seek the light.

We shape the world with dreams and schemes,
As woven threads unite our dreams.
In resonance, we find our ground,
With every thought, new paths abound.

So let us share, expand the fold,
With every whisper, stories told.
In resonance, forever we thrive,
Ideas give the heart its drive.

Sculpting the Air

With gentle hands, we shape the breeze,
In every sigh, the spirit frees.
The air, a canvas, waiting still,
To hold our dreams, our deepest will.

Each breath we take, a mark we make,
In sculpted forms that light will wake.
The whispers rise, as colors swirl,
In fragrant notes, our thoughts unfurl.

To mold the silence into sound,
In every heartbeat, life is found.
We craft with ease, our voices soar,
To dance upon the air we pour.

The sculptor's touch is soft and true,
With every breath, we start anew.
In harmony, we find our place,
As we embrace the open space.

So let us breathe, and let it flow,
In sculpted air, our visions grow.
For in the lightness, we may find,
The art of life, forever kind.

Seeds of Creativity

In the garden of the mind,
Ideas bloom in colors bright,
Each thought a seed, unique yet intertwined,
Growing under the sun's warm light.

Whispers of dreams begin to sprout,
Nurtured by the care we sow,
With each doubt cast out, no room for doubt,
In rich soil, our imaginations grow.

From tiny thoughts, the wonders rise,
A tapestry spun from our heart's desires,
Boundless visions take to the skies,
Fanning flames of our innermost fires.

Through trials, we seek what is true,
Watered by passion, we chase the stars,
Bringing forth creations anew,
Turning our scars into art that's ours.

So plant your seeds, let them take root,
For creativity knows no bounds,
In every heart, a gentle flute,
Playing the song of the earth's sounds.

Beyond the Horizon of Thought

Waves of contemplation rise,
Breaking softly on shores of mind,
Beyond the horizon, the truth lies,
Waiting patiently for us to find.

Ideas drift like clouds in the sky,
Shifting colors, forming new shapes,
In the silence, we learn to fly,
Past the limits of mental tapes.

Each question a star, bright and bold,
Illuminating paths in the night,
Through the dark, our visions unfold,
Guiding us to the dawn's first light.

With courage, we journey forth,
Exploring the depths of our being,
Casting dreams as our sturdy worth,
In the vastness, we find our seeing.

Beyond horizons, we seek the rays,
Of wisdom that sparkles and gleams,
Together we march through life's maze,
For in unity, we weave our dreams.

The Melody of Possibility

In every note, a chance unfolds,
Harmonies blend, creating more,
The rhythm of life in stories told,
Echoing softly from shore to shore.

With every chord, potential sings,
A symphony waits to be born,
In the stillness, the heart takes wings,
In the quiet dawn, ideas are worn.

Let the music guide our way,
Through valleys of doubt, over hills of fear,
In the dance of the mind, we sway,
To the melody only we can hear.

With each refrain, we grow and change,
Exploring the depths where dreams reside,
In the vast realm, so wild and strange,
The melody carries us, a faithful guide.

Together we weave these threads of sound,
In possibility's embrace, we find release,
Creating a world where dreams abound,
Where every note plays a part of peace.

Illuminated Pathways

In the twilight, paths appear,
Guided by stars, we take our stride,
Each step revealing what's held dear,
With every heartbeat, the world's wide.

Footprints glimmer on the ground,
Echoes of journeys past and new,
Through shadows where light is found,
Hope blooms bright, painting the view.

The lantern of dreams lights the way,
Illuminating fears that fade,
Every choice a dance of play,
In the glow, our spirits are made.

On these pathways, stories intertwine,
Lessons learned in the flickering glow,
With courage, our hearts align,
In the light of understanding, we grow.

As we wander these illuminated trails,
Together we forge a destiny bright,
Guided by love, where endless hope prevails,
In the embrace of the deepening night.

The Flight of Fancy

In the skies where dreams take flight,
Wings unfurl in morning light.
Silent whispers on the breeze,
Carried far with graceful ease.

Thoughts like feathers drift and soar,
Opening wide a hidden door.
Imagination, bold and bright,
Guides us through the endless night.

Clouds like castles, buoyant, white,
Woven threads of sheer delight.
Every heartbeat feels the grace,
As wonders form in boundless space.

Where the stars embrace the moon,
Hope is woven into tune.
Each horizon calls our name,
In this dance, we find our flame.

Let us chase where visions blend,
Not just dreams, but truths transcend.
In this flight, we find our way,
Crafting magic day by day.

Uncharted Realms

Beyond the map, where few have tread,
Lies a path where stories spread.
Mysteries wrapped in twilight's shroud,
Calling softly, strong yet loud.

Whispers echo through the trees,
Carried soft upon the breeze.
Each new dawn unveils a quest,
To explore where hearts find rest.

Mountains rise, and rivers flow,
Secrets of the earth bestow.
In the shadows, light breaks through,
Forming worlds both fresh and new.

With every step, a chance to find,
The beating pulse of humankind.
Adventure waits on every shore,
In uncharted realms, we uncover more.

So let us roam beyond the seen,
In the vast expanse, we glean.
Fuel the fire of wild desire,
In every heart, an endless choir.

Chasing the Invisible

Through the fog where silence dwells,
Echoes linger, time compels.
Thoughts like shadows, fleeting fast,
Whispers of a dream long cast.

In the corners of the mind,
Fragments of what we can find.
Chasing notions, soft as air,
Searching boldly, unaware.

What is seen and what is felt,
Lines of reason slowly melt.
Impressions left in fleeting grace,
The invisible takes its place.

Each moment a brushstroke true,
Painting life in shades of blue.
As we wander, hearts aligned,
In this chase, the truth we'll find.

Let us dive into the void,
Where reality's joy is toyed.
In the dance of light and shade,
Chasing dreams that will not fade.

Color in the Shadows

In the dusk where secrets play,
Colors dance at end of day.
Brushes dip in twilight's hue,
Painting tales both old and new.

Softly glows the amber light,
Illuminating silent night.
Every shadow tells a story,
In the dark, there's hidden glory.

Against the gray, bright hues ignite,
Life emerges, shining bright.
Even in the deep of dark,
Colors weave their quiet spark.

With each stroke, the world awakes,
Life's vibrance, music makes.
In stillness, we find our might,
Coloring shadows, pure delight.

So let the palette often blend,
In every curve, let colors mend.
Light and dark, a sacred dance,
In the shadows lies our chance.

Secrets of the Unbound

In shadows deep, the whispers cry,
A tale of wings that dare to fly.
Mysteries weave through silent nights,
Unlock the heart, unleash your sights.

Hidden paths in moonlit dreams,
Awaken thoughts in silver streams.
The secret world calls out your name,
To dance with life, ignite the flame.

In every pause, a truth is found,
Freedom's song in echoes sound.
With every step, let courage rise,
To chase the vast and endless skies.

The unbound spirit knows no fear,
Embrace the light, draw the near.
In every heartbeat, secrets blend,
A journey's start, the soul's ascend.

So dare to wander, seek and roam,
In every heart, you find a home.
The secrets known to those who seek,
Are stories told in whispers meek.

The Lighthouse of Ideas

Upon the shore, a beacon stands,
Casting rays from guiding hands.
Ideas twinkle like the stars,
A lighthouse shining near and far.

When storms of doubt begin to brew,
Its light will show the path that's true.
Each thought a wave upon the sea,
Inspire the hearts of you and me.

Within the walls of a quiet mind,
The brightest sparks are often blind.
But in this light, they find their way,
To guide the dreamers on their day.

Through fog and fear, the visions gleam,
In shadows thick, they breathe and dream.
Let creativity's fire ignite,
And paint the canvas in pure light.

So let your thoughts take flight and soar,
The lighthouse opens every door.
With every flicker, find your spark,
And let your ideas light the dark.

Symphony of the Soul

In the stillness, melodies rise,
A symphony that never lies.
Notes like whispers, soft and clear,
Resonate with what we hold dear.

Rhythms pulse in heartbeats strong,
Every sorrow finds a song.
Harmony woven through each tear,
A tapestry of joy and fear.

The orchestra of life unfolds,
With tales of warmth and dreams retold.
In every chord, a story lives,
A gift of all that music gives.

Let the winds of passion play,
Let every note share its say.
In unity, the echoes blend,
A symphony that knows no end.

Embrace the sound, let spirits soar,
The soul's own song forevermore.
In every silence, hear the call,
The symphony that binds us all.

The Dance of Inspiration

In fleeting moments, ideas bloom,
A dance of light that fills the room.
With every step, the mind takes flight,
Inspiration whispers in the night.

From ashes rise the brightest flames,
A waltz of dreams, no two the same.
Each twirl a chance to explore the new,
A canvas wide, with colors true.

With grace, the vision sways and spins,
In every heart, a spark begins.
The rhythm flows, ignites the soul,
A dance that makes the spirit whole.

Let creativity guide your feet,
In every stumble, feel the beat.
The dance of life, a swirling fate,
Embrace the magic while you wait.

So take my hand, let's move as one,
Together shining like the sun.
In every heartbeat, feel the chance,
To join the world in this grand dance.

The Garden of Possibilities

In the garden where dreams bloom bright,
Every seed tells a story, a whispered light.
Paths diverge, with choices to explore,
Hope dances freely, forever more.

Colors blend, a canvas so grand,
Nature's palette, crafted by hand.
Winds carry secrets of love and fate,
In this space, we dare to create.

Sunshine kisses the tender ground,
In every silence, inspiration is found.
Little wonders arise from the soil,
In this haven, we courageously toil.

The fragrance of dreams fills the air,
Every corner, a reason to care.
Blossoms twirl in the gentle breeze,
A sanctuary, where hearts find ease.

So wander freely, let your spirit soar,
In the garden of life, there's always more.
Turn every stone, uncover what's true,
The possibilities await, just for you.

Reflections in the Mirror of Dreams

Glimmers of hope in a twilight haze,
Mirrors reflect our untold days.
Shadows dance with whispered desires,
In the stillness, our soul inspires.

Each glance reveals a story untold,
Fragments of courage woven in gold.
Hopes entwined in the fabric of night,
Reflections flicker, igniting the light.

The mirror shows paths, both near and far,
Echoes of wishes, like a shooting star.
With every gaze, the future grows bright,
Our dreams take shape in the quiet night.

Dare to explore what the heart seeks,
In mirrored moments, the spirit speaks.
Journey within where the heart resides,
And find the strength where true magic hides.

So stand before it, open your mind,
In reflections, the answers you'll find.
Embrace the dreamer that still believes,
In the mirror of hope, the heart weaves.

The Art of Daydreaming

In the quiet corners of the mind,
Wonders begin, waiting to unwind.
Colors swirl in a gentle haze,
Lost in thought, in a soft embrace.

Time stretches thin on gossamer threads,
Imaginations soar, as reality sheds.
Each flicker of thought, a vivid delight,
Painting the day in shades so bright.

Clouds of whimsy float past with grace,
In daydreams, we find our sacred space.
A canvas blank, our spirits take flight,
In the realm of dreams, our hearts ignite.

Stories unfold in that timeless domain,
Adventures await, free from all pain.
In every heartbeat, a new tale awaits,
The art of daydreaming opens the gates.

So let your thoughts weave a tapestry bright,
In the garden of dreams, we're free to write.
Embrace the pause, let your spirit roam,
In daydream's embrace, we find our home.

Stars Within Reach

Under the vast, endless night sky,
Stars twinkle softly, whispering why.
Each one a dream, a wish cast free,
In the cosmos, we seek to be.

Galaxies swirl in a dance of light,
Connecting our hearts, igniting our sight.
With every glance, the universe beams,
A reminder that we're all part of dreams.

Comets streak by, like fleeting time,
Leaving behind stories, a rhythm, a rhyme.
In the canvas of dark, find your spark,
For in every night, there lies hope in the dark.

Reach out your hand, let your spirit soar,
For the stars above are forever more.
In their glow, find courage to chase,
Every desire, every dream, every place.

So gather your wishes, let them take flight,
For stars within reach shine brilliantly bright.
In the cosmic embrace, let your heart teach,
That dreams are alive when we reach for each.

Whispers of the Untold

In shadows where secrets play,
Soft murmurs drift and sway.
Stories locked in silent night,
Await the dawn's revealing light.

Echoes dance on midnight air,
Lifting tales beyond compare.
Fables hidden, waiting still,
In whispers, hearts begin to fill.

Ancient dreams take flight anew,
Carried by the wind so true.
Voices rise, a gentle call,
Inviting joy to touch us all.

Moments lost but never gone,
In each breath, a silent song.
Secrets woven, time forgot,
In the quiet, we are taught.

Unraveled threads of history,
In every sigh, a mystery.
Here we find what once was lost,
In whispers soft, we count the cost.

Canvas of Dreams

Brushstrokes of the night's embrace,
Colors dance in endless space.
Each hue tells a tale untold,
On this canvas, dreams unfold.

Stars flicker, a vibrant thread,
Woven where the heart is led.
Imagination takes its flight,
Painting worlds in soft twilight.

Moments captured, fleeting fast,
In this art, the die is cast.
Every vision, bold and bright,
Crafts the shadows into light.

Voices echo through the frame,
In this gallery of fame.
Life's adventures, bold and grand,
Brought to life with gentle hand.

In colors rich, we soar and glide,
In this world, our hopes reside.
Canvas wide, with dreams to share,
An endless journey, free as air.

Echoes of a Wandering Mind

Thoughts scatter like autumn leaves,
Drifting where the spirit weaves.
In quiet corners, whispers blend,
As journeys twist and softly bend.

Memories call from distant shores,
Unlocking all the hidden doors.
Each echo a reminder true,
Of all the places I once knew.

Questions linger like a breeze,
Riding on the swaying trees.
Wandering paths of what could be,
Map of dreams laid out for me.

In solitude, inspiration's found,
In fleeting thoughts that swirl around.
Each reflection, a vital sign,
Guiding me through the vast divine.

Through echoes clear, I start to seek,
The silences that speak unique.
A wandering mind, a free embrace,
Explores the depths of time and space.

Stars Within the Heart

In every pulse, a universe,
With galaxies that quietly converse.
Stars flicker deep within the soul,
Guiding us towards our goal.

Through the night, their light does shine,
Mapping paths where dreams align.
Each twinkle whispers from afar,
That we are never truly dark.

Infinite wonders in each glance,
Painting skies for hearts' romance.
Strong and bright, they hold our gaze,
Reminding us of brighter days.

In the void, a spark ignites,
A symphony of shining lights.
Together we can weave our fate,
With every star, we navigate.

So hold close these steadfast sparks,
For even in the deepest darks,
The stars within can guide us true,
As we explore the vast anew.

Breathing Life into Dreams

In the silence of the night, they gleam,
Whispers of hope, the heart's soft beam.
With every heartbeat, they come alive,
A canvas of wishes, where visions thrive.

Through valleys of doubt, they take flight,
Carried on wings of sheer delight.
A dance of promises, bold and bright,
Awakening souls in the still of night.

Every sigh a brushstroke, a spark,
Painting the shadows, igniting the dark.
For in dreams, a journey begins anew,
Chasing horizons, the world is our view.

When morning breaks, and reality calls,
These dreams weave through the moments, enthrall.
They ground us deep, yet lift us high,
Breathing life into hopes that never die.

So dare to dream, to imagine, to feel,
In the heart's quiet chambers, let magic reveal.
For life starts with dreams, and dreams can ignite,
The wonder unfolding in purest light.

Mindscapes of Endless Theories

In the labyrinth of thoughts, I roam,
Each corner hides a new unknown,
Questions swirl like shadows dance,
In the depths of pondering, I take a chance.

Concepts collide in a vivid stream,
Constructs of reason, the mind's grand scheme.
From chaos to order, the journey unfolds,
In the realms of wonder, knowledge beholds.

Through webs of wisdom, I trace the lines,
Connecting the dots where the cosmos shines.
Ideas like fireflies, flickering bright,
Illuminate the darkness, guide me to light.

With each hypothesis, I challenge the skies,
The thirst for answers, in truth I rise.
From the petty to profound, all things relate,
In this mindscape of theories, I contemplate.

So let the intellect roam unconfined,
In the vast expanse of the curious mind.
For every question holds a key,
To unlocking the mysteries of eternity.

The Fire of Curiosity

A flicker ignites, a spark in the night,
The flame of questions, burning bright.
With every glance, a world unfolds,
In the heart of inquisition, stories are told.

Craving the unknown, I wander far,
Chasing the tail of a distant star.
Learning from whispers of ages past,
Fueling the fire, an eternal cast.

In the warmth of wonder, I dare to explore,
Each layer of knowledge, I yearn to implore.
From microcosms to the vast expanse,
In every discovery, I find a chance.

The flame flickers gently, yet fiercely it burns,
In the dance of the curious, the heart yearns.
For the quest never ends, it's a beautiful race,
With every new question, I find my place.

So feed the fire with your dreams and your quests,
In the heart of the curious, adventure rests.
For curiosity's flame, unyielding and true,
Illuminates the path, forever anew.

Under the Velvet Sky

Beneath the vast, embracing night,
Stars twinkle softly, a wondrous sight.
Whispers of cosmos in every breeze,
Under the velvet, our hearts find ease.

Moonlight drapes like a silken cloak,
In its embrace, silent secrets spoke.
Dreamers gather, lost in their schemes,
Fleeting moments, like ethereal dreams.

In the stillness, time holds its breath,
As shadows dance with the dusk of death.
A canvas of colors, dusk to dawn,
Under the velvet, our spirits are drawn.

Every heartbeat echoes, a timeless song,
In the hush of the night, where we belong.
Together we linger, in starlit delight,
Finding our stories in the depths of the night.

So revel in wonder, let your soul fly,
Under the velvet of the night sky.
For in every glimmer, hope gently sighs,
A tapestry woven where destiny lies.

Capturing the Ether

In twilight's grasp, we chase the light,
Whispers of stars in the deepening night.
Moments preserved in a fragile embrace,
Echoes of time in a timeless space.

Clouds drift softly, painting the sky,
Colors that dance, as the day waves goodbye.
Fleeting glances of a universe wide,
After the dusk and the evening tide.

Voices of dreams in the ether we weave,
Stories untold that the heart can perceive.
In the silence, a symphony plays,
Carried by breezes through luminous rays.

Caught in the shimmer of celestial glow,
We navigate paths where the wild wonders flow.
With every heartbeat, we seek and explore,
Filling our souls with the cosmos' lore.

Here in the twilight, our spirits take flight,
Capturing beauty in the magic of night.
With stardust and dreams, we'll forever remain,
Chasing the ether, through joy and through pain.

The Lab of Dreams

In a room filled with whispers, ideas ignite,
Curious minds turn the dark into light.
Potions of thought bubble, shimmer, and blend,
Crafting the futures we dream to transcend.

Sketches of wonders on tattered old sheets,
Blueprints of journeys where magic completes.
In the lab of the heart, where visions align,
Imagination flourishes, boldly divine.

Fragments of wishes float through the air,
Chasing the shadows, dissolving despair.
Here laughter erupts, and silence sings sweet,
Each moment a treasure, each heartbeat a beat.

Beneath the bright glow of flickering flame,
The spirits of dreamers are calling our names.
Like alchemists turning mere dreams into gold,
We fashion our stories, both gentle and bold.

In this endless quest where ideas take flight,
We sculpt the impossible out of pure light.
So step into this realm of boundless delight,
Together we weave the wildest of sight.

The Weavers of Wonder

With threads of starlight, we craft and we spin,
Tales of enchantment, where journeys begin.
Each strand a story, each color a song,
In the loom of existence, where we all belong.

We gather the whispers of worlds yet unseen,
Stitching the fabric of what might have been.
Golden horizons and shadows of dreams,
We dance through the echoes, unravel the seams.

In this tapestry rich with laughter and tears,
Weaved by the hands of our hopes and our fears.
Magic entwined in the fibers of fate,
Creating a canvas with love, never late.

The weavers of wonder, with hearts open wide,
Invite all the dreamers to dance by our side.
Together we fashion the threads of the night,
Binding the restless to bask in the light.

So gather your thoughts as we spin and entwine,
In the workshop of wonder, through shadows we shine.
Crafting the moments, both fleeting and true,
In the weavers of wonder, there's magic in you.

Secrets of the Dreamweavers

In twilight whispers, shadows dance,
Threads of vision, a fleeting glance.
Weaving tales of dusk and dawn,
In realms where all of time has drawn.

Beneath the moon's caress so bright,
A tapestry of stars takes flight.
Each dream a secret, softly spun,
In the silence, we are one.

Voices linger, echoing clear,
Mysteries held, yet drawing near.
With every sigh, a world unfolds,
In realms where everyone beholds.

Fleeting moments capture hearts,
In woven dreams, reality departs.
Through veils of night, we find our way,
In dreams where shadows gently play.

So let us wander, hand in hand,
Through whispered paths in wonderland.
The secrets kept, forever gleam,
In the sacred art of the dream.

Enchanted Thoughts

Drifting softly on a breeze,
Thoughts entwined among the trees.
Whispers echo in the air,
Magic lingers everywhere.

Each reflection, a sparkle bright,
Dancing flames in the velvet night.
Moments captured, dreams unfurl,
In the heart of a mystic whirl.

In twilight's glow, the secrets bloom,
All the stars begin to loom.
Painting skies with gentle hues,
As ideas drift, we choose and muse.

Through the mist, our spirits roam,
In enchanted realms, we find our home.
With every thought, a story spun,
In a world where dreams are won.

So let us wander, free of weight,
With every breath, we celebrate.
In the magic of each thought we weave,
A tapestry of dreams, believe.

The Alchemy of Wonder

In the heart of night, dreams are born,
A golden light, the world adorns.
Transforming shadows into art,
In every whisper, a tender start.

With every moment, time distills,
The essence of our greatest thrills.
A potion brewed from love and light,
Infusing magic into the night.

In this dance of stars so bright,
We find the truth in pure delight.
Crafting joy from every tear,
The alchemy of hope draws near.

Breaking barriers, setting free,
In the wonder of you and me.
A spark ignites, and passions flow,
In the light of dreams, we grow.

So let us gather, heart to heart,
In this alchemy, we play our part.
With every step, we create,
A world transformed, a wondrous fate.

Labyrinths of the Soul

In the depths where shadows dwell,
A whisper echoes, a distant bell.
Twists and turns that never cease,
In the maze, we seek our peace.

Through corridors of light and shade,
Each step forward, a choice is made.
Faces linger, memories call,
In the labyrinth, we rise and fall.

With every path, a story grows,
In the silence, understanding flows.
The heart beats louder, clear and true,
In this journey, I find you.

Lost and found in the sacred space,
Embracing time, the soul's embrace.
Through winding roads, we learn to dance,
In the depths, we find our chance.

So take my hand, let's lose the fright,
Together we'll explore the night.
In labyrinths of the soul we'll stroll,
Discovering wonders that make us whole.

Ripples of Imagination

In the stillness of the night,
Dreams take flight, soft and bright.
Waves of thoughts begin to flow,
Echoes of what we long to know.

Colors dance upon the stream,
Whispers weaving through the dream.
Each ripple tells a tale anew,
A world that's painted just for you.

Beneath the surface, secrets hide,
Unlocking fantasies inside.
With every thought, a spark ignites,
Illuminating shadowy sights.

As dawn breaks with a gentle sigh,
The ripples fade, but dreams don't die.
In the heart, they find their way,
To live again another day.

So close your eyes and feel the sway,
Of imagination's graceful play.
For in that world, we can escape,
Forever crafting our own fate.

The Brushstrokes of Reality

A canvas stretched, so wide and bare,
Life's palette waits, with colors rare.
Each brushstroke tells a story true,
Painting moments, old and new.

With every hue, we mark our place,
A fleeting glimpse of time and space.
Each line a choice, each curve a dream,
Reality flows, a flowing stream.

Sometimes bold, sometimes soft and shy,
The brushstrokes whisper, never lie.
In shadows deep, in light so bright,
We find our path, we chase our light.

From vibrant reds to tranquil blue,
We capture life in every hue.
The canvas breathes as we create,
A masterpiece that bears our weight.

So take the brush, let spirit soar,
With every stroke, explore and explore.
For in this art, we find what's real,
A gallery of how we feel.

Sparkling Chimeras

Dreams like fireflies in the night,
Flit and flicker, a wondrous sight.
Chimeras dance on golden streams,
Guiding us through our wildest dreams.

With shimmering wings, they soar so high,
Tracing paths across the sky.
Each spark a promise, a wish to hold,
Stories crafted, treasures untold.

In the twilight, shadows play,
Casting visions that sway and sway.
Each flicker brings a secret glance,
A world alive with every chance.

These sparkling forms, they weave and spin,
Crafting magic, drawing us in.
In their glow, we dare to seek,
The beauty in the soft and weak.

So chase the light, let wonders call,
Embrace the chimeras, one and all.
For in their dance, we find the spark,
Illuminating corners dark.

The Canvas of Possibilities

A wide expanse of open space,
Invites the heart to dream and chase.
With every stroke, a path unfolds,
A realm of wonders yet untold.

From vibrant shades of hope and fear,
To muted tones that draw us near.
Possibilities intertwine and weave,
In this canvas, we believe.

Brush to canvas, hopes arise,
Visions dancing in our eyes.
Each line invites a fresh embrace,
A journey through this wondrous place.

Within these bounds, our spirits play,
Creating futures from the gray.
With every choice, a new design,
A tapestry, both yours and mine.

So take a chance, let colors bloom,
Transform the silence into room.
For on this canvas, life will sing,
The endless joy that dreaming brings.

Dreamscapes and Journeys

In shadows soft, the dreams take flight,
They weave through stars, the silent night.
On whispered winds, adventures call,
In twisted paths, we rise and fall.

Through forests deep, where echoes play,
With every breath, we drift away.
In realms unknown, our spirits glide,
A dance of hope where fears abide.

Beneath the moon's enchanting glow,
The heart awakes, the mind will flow.
A tapestry of starry beams,
In dreamscapes bright, we find our dreams.

A journey's end, yet still we roam,
With every step, we call it home.
In every truth, in every lie,
In journeys vast, we learn to fly.

Eternal tales in silence spun,
In dreamscapes wide, we chase the sun.
With every heartbeat, life unfurls,
In hidden paths, our vision swirls.

Uncharted Thoughts

In corners dark, where shadows sleep,
The thoughts arise, both wild and deep.
They twist and turn, a frantic race,
In uncharted lands, we find our place.

With every doubt, a chance to grow,
The whispers wrap like winter's snow.
In tangled webs, we set our sights,
On paths unseen, in endless nights.

Each notion born, a spark ignites,
In restless minds, the heart ignites.
A canvas blank, where dreams take shape,
In uncharted realms, we dare escape.

Through misty trails, the visions soar,
On gentle waves, we seek the shore.
With every risk, we learn to trust,
In uncharted thoughts, we find the dust.

And as we wander, free and bold,
The stories bloom, the truths unfold.
In every heart, a tale once sought,
In uncharted lands, we find our thought.

The Power of Reverie

In twilight's glow, the mind will bend,
To visions sweet that never end.
With every sigh, the fantasies rise,
In power's grip, we touch the skies.

A world apart, where wonders lay,
In reverie's grasp, we drift away.
With colors bright, we paint our dreams,
In silence, hear the spirit's screams.

The heart ignites, a flame anew,
In whispered secrets, we break through.
With every pulse, a journey starts,
In power's reign, we share our hearts.

Through airy realms, the whispers flow,
In shimmering light, we seek to grow.
With each soft thought, the magic flows,
In reverie's arms, the spirit glows.

A tapestry of hope and fear,
In dreams we find, our path is clear.
With every vision, strong and free,
In power's grasp, we find our glee.

Painting with Words

With every stroke, a tale unfolds,
In whispered lines, the heart retolds.
A brush of ink on paper white,
In colors bright, we chase the light.

Each word a petal, soft and rare,
In gardens lush, we tend with care.
With every phrase, a world is born,
In silence deep, our dreams are sworn.

Through shadows cast, the stories play,
In echoes sweet, they find their way.
With every verse, a canvas wide,
In painting's grace, the muse will guide.

A swirl of thoughts, a dance divine,
In vibrant hues, our souls align.
With brushes bold, we create the skies,
In painted worlds, our spirit flies.

With every line, a heartbeat's song,
In swirling colors, we belong.
With words the shade, with thoughts the frame,
In painting songs, we carve our name.

The Portal of Creativity

In the stillness of thought's embrace,
Ideas emerge, a gentle trace.
Whispers of dreams in colors bright,
Spark a flame, igniting the night.

With every stroke of a brush or pen,
A world takes shape, again and again.
Boundless realms await to explore,
As visions dance on the mind's floor.

Through pathways woven with threads of light,
Inspiration flows, a pure delight.
Unlocking doors to the unseen,
Where fantasies dwell and glories glean.

A symphony of thoughts intertwine,
In the heart of chaos, order aligns.
Creativity blooms like flowers in spring,
A celebration of all that we bring.

Within this portal, time stands still,
With every heartbeat, a vibrant thrill.
Come, step inside, let your heart guide,
In the realm of dreams, let imagination ride.

Seeds of Innovation

In the soil of thoughts, ideas sprout,
Imaginations roam, weaving about.
Tiny whispers of change take hold,
In the quiet, new wonders unfold.

Curiosity ignites the spark,
A journey begins, traversing the dark.
Cultivating visions with patience and grace,
Nurturing dreams in a sacred space.

From every challenge, a lesson learned,
Seeds of wisdom in fires burned.
With courage to question, to break the mold,
Innovations bloom, turning to gold.

Collaboration blossoms, hands intertwine,
Together we rise, a shared design.
In the garden of progress, we sow,
Reaping the fruits of what our minds know.

As cycles turn and seasons change,
The seeds we've planted begin to range.
In the heart of our efforts, we find the way,
To shape the future from the dreams of today.

The Resolution of Daydreams

In the realm of thoughts, we softly drift,
With daydreams as gifts, a cherished lift.
Bound by nothing, our spirits roam,
In fleeting moments, we find our home.

Lost in stories that dance on air,
Imaginary journeys take us there.
Where wishes bloom in radiant hues,
And hope enchants with every muse.

With every daydream, new paths arise,
A tapestry woven with laughter and sighs.
In the embrace of possibilities vast,
We discover our worth, the shadows cast.

As horizons expand beyond the known,
In daydreams, the seeds of resolve are sown.
A canvas of purpose, we paint with light,
Transforming visions into sheer delight.

So let us dream, unbound and free,
For in our hearts, we hold the key.
With every resolution, we ignite the flame,
In the world of daydreams, we're never the same.

Embers of Enlightenment

In the quiet echoes of midnight's breath,
Wisdom glimmers, defying death.
Embers stir in the depths of the soul,
Illuminating paths, making us whole.

Through shadows long, we seek the light,
In the fire of thought, we stand upright.
Each spark a lesson, each glow a sign,
Awakening truths, eternally divine.

In the dance of knowledge, we find our place,
With open hearts, we embrace the chase.
Questioning all, with courage finite,
For enlightenment's flame burns ever bright.

With every step on this sacred ground,
The whispers of ages in silence resound.
Through struggles faced and battles won,
In the embers of wisdom, we are one.

So gather 'round the warmth of the fire,
In its embrace, let your soul aspire.
For enlightenment's journey never ends,
In the heart of every seeker, it transcends.

The Proxy of Thoughts

In shadows deep where whispers flow,
A mind's vast realm, a quiet show.
Thoughts dance like leaves on autumn's air,
They soar and dive, both bold and rare.

Dreams catch the light, a fleeting spark,
Each notion glows, igniting the dark.
In silence, secrets twist and twine,
A tapestry woven with threads divine.

Echoes linger, fading then bright,
Each pulse of reason, a guiding light.
In quiet corners, truths emerge,
A symphony born from inner surge.

Through tangled paths, ideas race,
Voices collide, a thrilling chase.
In the labyrinth, clarity shines,
Minds intertwine, crafting designs.

So let the thoughts like rivers flow,
In depths profound, let learning grow.
Waves of perception, vast and wide,
In the proxy of thought, we abide.

Bridge to the Beyond

A bridge of dreams in starlit night,
Connecting realms, both dark and bright.
With every step, the past unwinds,
To futures vast, where hope aligns.

Voices call from shores unknown,
In whispers soft, seeds of wisdom sown.
With courage bold, we take our stand,
As fate awaits with open hand.

The skies unfold, a canvas clear,
With brushstroke paths that persevere.
Across the void, visions gleam,
A bridge of thought, a living dream.

In moments shared, the heart expands,
Uniting souls, in trust it stands.
Together we leap, into the vast,
Bound by the ties of future and past.

So walk the bridge, let spirit soar,
In every heartbeat, find the door.
To realms beyond, where dreams come true,
A journey painted in every hue.

Infinite Echoes

In chambers deep, where echoes play,
Thoughts reverberate, night and day.
Each whisper holds a world inside,
Infinite paths where dreams collide.

Through time's embrace, the past resounds,
In every heartbeat, history founds.
Lessons learned from ages past,
In echoes soft, shadows are cast.

Voices linger on the breeze,
In every rustle of the trees.
They're stories told, yet untold still,
In silent places, hearts can thrill.

Rippled moments, like stones in streams,
Create a tapestry of dreams.
Each echo carries weight and grace,
Transforming time, each sacred space.

So listen close to the sounds around,
In every echo, wisdom's found.
An infinite loop of life unfurled,
In echoes deep, we shape our world.

The Spell of Inspiration

When twilight falls and stars ignite,
A spell is cast, weaving the night.
With every breath, creativity flows,
In silence deep, the magic grows.

Words take flight on wings of dreams,
In flickering lights, imagination beams.
From depths unknown, ideas arise,
A surge of wonder, a sweet surprise.

With every stroke, the canvas beams,
A masterpiece born from whispered dreams.
Colors dance, a vivid blend,
The heart's own voice, each line a friend.

In sparks of thought, the world awakes,
Through art and heart, the magic takes.
A gentle nudge from muse divine,
In inspiration's grip, our spirits shine.

So heed the call when silence reigns,
For in that space, the heart contains.
The spell of inspiration ever near,
Awakening dreams, igniting cheer.

The Spark of Wonder

In the cradle of night, stars align,
Whispers of dreams begin to entwine.
Curiosity dances, a flickering flame,
Each new discovery, a journey to claim.

Eyes wide with joy, the unknown calls,
A flicker of hope in the darkest halls.
Moments of magic unfold like a flower,
Nature's own canvas, a source of power.

Through the laughter of children, a world is bright,
Imagination soars, taking delightful flight.
Every question a key, unlocking our way,
In the spark of wonder, we boldly play.

Time and again, we're drawn to the light,
The essence of life in each day and night.
Bound by the quest, we dare to explore,
The spark of wonder, forever we'll adore.

In unity and joy, our spirits ignite,
Journeying together, fueled by delight.
With hearts open wide, we chase after dreams,
In the dance of wonder, nothing's as it seems.

Mosaics of the Mind

Fragments of thoughts, a colorful scene,
Shattered reflections, what might have been.
Cascading moments, harmony found,
In the tapestry woven, our truths abound.

Each piece tells a story, unique in its way,
Mirrors of laughter, heartaches on display.
Colors of chaos, patterns unseen,
Mosaics of the mind, where we've been.

Memories linger like paint on the wall,
In shades of the past, we rise and we fall.
Fragments of time, stitched into tonight,
As we navigate shadows, searching for light.

The mind's vibrant landscape, a beautiful mess,
Every thought a brushstroke, creating finesse.
In understanding others, we find our own grace,
Through mosaics of the mind, we embrace.

Together we dance through the puzzles we face,
Interwoven lives in a shared, sacred space.
In the art of connection, we come alive,
In mosaics of the mind, we thrive.

Cascades of Creation

From whispers of thought, ideas cascade,
In the heart of the artist, dreams are displayed.
Colors collide in a glorious spin,
As cascades of creation begin to begin.

Each drop of passion, a vibrant new hue,
From silence erupts a harmonic breakthrough.
Rhythms of life flow through every vein,
In the pools of our spirit, joy accommodates pain.

With every new layer, horizons expand,
The artistry blossoming, fresh and unplanned.
In the dance of creation, we grow and we learn,
Cascading visions, in our hearts they burn.

Spirals of wonder enrapture the eye,
In the forge of the moment, we reach for the sky.
With each stroke of brilliance, our souls we ignite,
In the cascades of creation, we see the light.

Together we gather, the dreamers unite,
Hands joined in purpose, our futures shine bright.
In the magic of making, our spirits take flight,
In cascades of creation, we find our delight.

Horizons of the Heart

Beneath endless skies, possibilities bloom,
Waves of affection, dispelling all gloom.
In the silence of night, whispers depart,
Guiding our journeys, horizons of the heart.

Through valleys of sorrow, we seek to ascend,
In bonds that grow deeper, we learn to mend.
The warmth of connection, a beacon of light,
In horizons of the heart, everything feels right.

Love's gentle embrace, a treasure to hold,
In stories of courage, our pasts unfold.
With each step we take, a new path unfolds,
Horizons of the heart, where joy overflows.

Trust like a river, flows ever so free,
In the depths of our being, we find unity.
With dreams intertwined, through the dark and the bright,

Horizons of the heart carry us through the night.

In the tapestry woven, our spirits align,
Together we wander, through love we define.
Each heartbeat a promise, each smile a start,
In the vastness of life, horizons of the heart.

Awakening the Muse

In silence deep, she stirs anew,
With whispers soft, dreams seek their cue.
A canvas waits, untouched, so bright,
As colors dance in morning light.

The heart in rhythm, pulses fierce,
Through shadows cast, her voice will pierce.
A tapestry of thoughts unwind,
Unlocking worlds within the mind.

A gentle push, a guiding hand,
In fleeting moments, ideas expand.
Embrace the spark, let visions flow,
For art is born where passions grow.

With every brush, a story weaves,
In twilight's glow, the spirit grieves.
Yet through the pain, creation sings,
With each new note, the heart takes wings.

Awakening now, the muse ignites,
A journey past the endless nights.
With fervent fire, she lights the way,
In fields of dreams, we'll dance and play.

Shattered Norms

In rigid lines, the world conforms,
Yet hearts aspire to break the storms.
With fervent cries, dreams clash and clash,
Defying fate, they boldly dash.

Through walls of doubt, we carve our way,
Where voices echo and shadows sway.
For in the cracks of societal chains,
Lies the spirit that forever reigns.

Traditions bound in iron grips,
But hope persists through countless trips.
With every challenge, courage grows,
As petals bloom from bitter throes.

A chorus rises, fierce and free,
In unity, we find the key.
To shatter norms and rewrite the tale,
As barriers break, we shall not fail.

Inired and brave, we stand as one,
Awakening truths, the battle begun.
To dance on shards of the old, grey stone,
In vibrant hues, we'll find our own.

The Symphony of Ideas

A melody of thoughts entwined,
In harmony, our dreams aligned.
Each note a whisper, bold and clear,
As visions rise, we draw them near.

With every beat, the heart resounds,
In quietude, the muse surrounds.
Ideas flow like rivers wide,
In symphonies, our souls abide.

In echoes bright, we find our song,
A place where every heart belongs.
With voices raised, we weave our fate,
Creating worlds that resonate.

The palette spreads, colors collide,
A canvas vast, with dreams inside.
As rhythms pulse and visions merge,
In unison, our passions surge.

A symphony that knows no bounds,
In every silence, music sounds.
With hand in hand, our spirits soar,
In the symphony of ideas, we explore.

Dancing with Shadows

In the twilight glow, they sway,
Whispers of night come out to play.
Silhouettes twirl on the dampened ground,
Echoes of dreams in silence found.

A flicker of light, a gentle breeze,
Shadows stretch and twist with ease.
Their graceful moves, a secret dance,
Entwined in fate, they find their chance.

Stars above watch the steps unfold,
Memories hidden, stories retold.
Each movement speaks, a silent cry,
If only the night would never die.

Embrace the dark, let it reside,
In shadows deep, where hopes abide.
They gather close, a timeless bond,
In every pulse, we learn to respond.

So dance on late, till the dawn breaks,
With shadows close, a trust that makes.
In every glide, there's a story shared,
A harmony found, in love declared.

The Alchemy of Now

Time funnels through the open hands,
Moments blend like shifting sands.
Now is but a fleeting breath,
A spark of life, the dance of death.

In stillness, truths begin to gleam,
Fragments woven into a dream.
Herein lies the treasure we seek,
In simple whispers that softly speak.

As seconds dissolve, they softly pour,
A canvas bright, we can't ignore.
Each heartbeat a reminder clear,
That magic brews within our sphere.

In laughter shared and tears that flow,
Alchemy shapes what we can't know.
Transform the mundane to divine,
With every second, let your soul shine.

Breathe in the now, let go of time,
Each moment lived is truly sublime.
In the dance of time, let spirits rise,
For here lies the truth, and the ultimate prize.

Threads of Wonder

In the fabric of night, tales are spun,
Threads of wonder, where dreams run.
Each stitch whispers secrets untold,
Of adventures vast and treasures bold.

Patterns form in the still of time,
With every hue, a reason to climb.
The weave of life, so intricate,
In every loop, we celebrate fate.

From the loom of moments, we create,
A tapestry rich, we contemplate.
Threads twine together, both bright and dim,
Crafting a story that's filled to the brim.

In the art of living, threads intertwine,
With colors vibrant, our spirits align.
Each flicker of joy, each sorrow's hue,
Shapes the portrait we carry through.

So gather your threads, weave them with care,
In the loom of your heart, let love declare.
Each wonder speaks, as the world spins on,
In every thread, a spark of dawn.

Kaleidoscope of Visions

A whirl of colors spins and sways,
Fragments of life in wondrous ways.
Through the lens, the world's delight,
Shifting forms, both dark and bright.

In every turn, new patterns emerge,
A vivid dance, where souls converge.
Dreams kaleidoscope, reward the heart,
In every glimpse, a brand new start.

Shards of memories, reflections blend,
In vibrant hues, they twist and bend.
A journey bound by hues alive,
In this mosaic, we learn to thrive.

Hold tight the visions, as they unfold,
In swirling tales, both new and old.
Every perspective, a life's embrace,
A kaleidoscope holds infinite grace.

So gaze upon the shifting frame,
As colors meld, it's never the same.
In the dance of light, we find our prize,
A spectrum of beauty in our eyes.

Serendipity's Touch

In the whisper of the night,
Stars collide in silent flight.
Moments dance, a chance embrace,
Fate unfolds with gentle grace.

Winds carry secrets from afar,
Guiding dreams like a shooting star.
Unexpected joys we find,
In the tapestry of the mind.

Paths cross in the golden hour,
Each heartbeat a blooming flower.
Fortune smiles, a soft caress,
Leading us to happiness.

Life's map is drawn in lines unclear,
Yet every turn brings us near.
Embrace the twists, the sudden bends,
For every road may lead to friends.

With serendipity in sight,
We dance beneath the starlit night.
Hold close the magic, let it stay,
As we wander on our way.

A Tapestry of Whimsy

Threads of laughter weave through time,
In a world adorned with rhyme.
Colors burst in joyful play,
A tapestry of dreams each day.

Clouds transform, a playful show,
Where imaginations freely flow.
Chasing shadows, colors bright,
Every turn a new delight.

Fluttering wings, a glimpse of cheer,
In every moment, magic near.
Curious hearts, with childlike glee,
Wander through our reverie.

In the garden of the mind,
Whimsy blooms, the rarest kind.
Fluttering leaves, a playful catch,
In a world where dreams can hatch.

Through laughter's embrace, we find our way,
Spinning stories penned in play.
Join the dance of the whimsical,
In the realm of the fantastical.

The Enchanted Mind

In shadows deep, where secrets dwell,
Whispers of magic cast their spell.
A labyrinth of thoughts unwind,
In the corners of the enchanted mind.

Stories live in every sigh,
Dreams take wing, they soar and fly.
With every thought, a world ignites,
In the realm of unseen sights.

Echoes of laughter linger still,
In the quiet, a gentle thrill.
Every moment, a spark divine,
Illuminating the mystic line.

As moonlight spills, and stars ascend,
Imagination knows no end.
With each heartbeat, a tale is spun,
In the mind's embrace, we become one.

Explore the depths, the heights, the bends,
In magic, reality blends.
For in the heart of every dream,
Lies the beauty of the unseen.

Fables from the Inner Realm

In the heart where stories bloom,
Lies a treasure in each room.
Fables whisper in the night,
Guiding souls with soft invite.

Creatures dance in shadows' grace,
Every tale finds its place.
From ancient lore to modern plights,
The inner realm ignites the nights.

A tapestry of voices sing,
Of hopes and dreams, the joys they bring.
In silence deep, a story thrives,
A mirror where the spirit dives.

With every heartbeat, lessons grow,
In the stories that we sow.
Wisdom shared through laughter's well,
Fables spun with magic's spell.

So gather close, the tales unfold,
In whispers soft, the truths retold.
For in the realm where fables live,
Is a gift that time will ever give.